THE WORD
FROM
THE CROSS

THE WORD FROM THE CROSS

RICHARD O. HOYER

CONCORDIA PUBLISHING HOUSE

SAINT LOUIS · LONDON

Concordia Publishing House, St. Louis, Missouri

Concordia Publishing House Ltd., London, E. C. 1

© 1968 Concordia Publishing House

Library of Congress Catalog Card No. 68-11894

CONTENTS

DEDICATED TO THE FAITHFUL
OF MOUNT GREENWOOD LUTHERAN CHURCH

whom the world calls fools
but whom God calls saints
and I call my brethren

PREFACE

The crucifixion and death of Jesus of Nazareth we believe and confess to be not the tragic lynching of a martyr but God in action saving the world He so loved. But whenever God acts He calls through that action to the lonely and the empty, inviting, urging, welcoming them home to Himself and to wholeness and fulfillment. Every act of God is a call.

So the Good Word about what happened on the cross is never only a message informing us about this once-for-all, overwhelming act of God's grace. The news of His saving act becomes the means by which the eternal Father calls to Himself those who will believe.

The sermons in this series seek not only to proclaim the Good Word *about* the cross, but to voice the Word *from* the cross, the call of God to sinners to come home. They are intended not only to show what God has done for us, but to show what God seeks to do through those who have heard and answered the call from the cross. They

7

try to provide the Holy Spirit with the means to call and put into action the saints of God.

Sermons are never more than a brother seeking to help a brother in the name of our one Lord and Savior. It is always amazing what God can do with the simple words of His people. May He use these, too.

RICHARD O. HOYER

Chicago, Illinois

1

The Word from the Cross:

Father, Forgive

ASH WEDNESDAY

Remember, O man, that "dust thou art and unto dust shalt thou return." With these ancient words reminding us of our mortality and of the sin which caused it, we with millions of our brothers and sisters throughout the world enter again the season of Lent. We begin again to watch with Christ in His suffering, to stand beside Him in His agony, to be with Him through the valley of the shadow of death. It is the least we can do. After all, we are the ones who caused His suffering; we made it all necessary. It is most fitting that the first day of Lent should be called Ash Wednesday, reminding us of the medieval practice of sprinkling ashes on the heads of penitents who wished to be restored to the fellowship of the church. For if there is one thing that Lent makes clear to us, it is our need for ashes, our need for penitence, and, above all, our need for forgiveness. The first word our Lord spoke from the cross is a word that forgives!

> And when they came to the place which is called The Skull, there they crucified Him, and the criminals, one on the right and one on the left. And Jesus said, "Father, forgive them; for they know not what they do."   LUKE 23:33-34

Father, forgive! Even while they are nailing Him to the rough timbers and the pain seethes through His body, He asks that those who nailed Him there might be forgiven — that we might be forgiven.

I. We Need Forgiveness

We need forgiveness. Indeed we do. But in all honesty we must ask, "For what? What sins do we feel we have done that need to be forgiven?" We can all make a long list of those. We can list things like drinking too much, greed, lust, stealing, cheating, selfishness, hurting others, losing our temper, and so on. But the trouble with making a long list like this is that these are only symptoms. We never really face the disease itself that's behind all these symptoms and causes them. But our Lord Jesus, in His first Word from the cross, clearly describes the situation: "Father, forgive them, for they don't know what they're doing."

Because We Don't Know What We're Doing

The soldiers, driving the rusty spikes through His hands and feet, didn't know what they were really doing — to them this was just the execution of another Jew. The leaders of Israel who had insisted on this execution did so in stubborn blindness, fully convinced, I am sure, that they were doing the will of God. The people of the world who on that morning were going about life as usual didn't know what was happening — that here the Creator was offering Himself as a sacrifice for His creatures. They didn't know what they were doing. How painfully clear that makes our disease to us! It's like a person who gets swamped with work and everything goes wrong until finally he cries out in despair, "I don't know what I'm

12

doing anymore!" He is confused, disorganized, and *utterly lost*. That really shows the disease of sin. The word "sin" does not just describe this long list of bad things we do and good things we don't do. It is a description of this lostness, this emptiness, this futility, this despair, this opposition to God and all His ways, which is revealed by our Lord's words, "They don't know what they're doing."

Because We Have Separated Ourselves from Our Father

We don't know what we're doing because we have separated ourselves from our Father. Adam and Eve walked away from God and said, "We can do without You." And don't we do the same thing still? So often when we walk away from the house of God to our homes, our jobs, our bowling alleys, or wherever we go, we don't take Him along. He's not at all involved. We seem to think we can get along perfectly well without Him. But we can't! Look at the mess we make of life. It is a time for ashes! Father, forgive us, for we don't know what we're doing! And even when we know, we can't seem to help ourselves.

Indeed we really walk away from Him because we oppose Him. God created a perfect world and made people live together in perfect love and harmony and bliss. It is His will that the world be a paradise, a Garden of Eden. But we don't know what we're doing! We have wrecked and continue

13

to wreck the whole thing. We oppose God's will. We go around hurting ourselves and others. We steal, we loot, we lie and cheat, we hurt and kill, we are mean and cruel — and what has happened to our paradise? It is a time for ashes! A time for us to be saying, "Father, forgive us, for we don't know what we're doing." And even when we know, we can't seem to stop ourselves.

Besides all this we also hide when He calls us, like Adam and Eve hiding behind fig-leaf aprons and bushes. We have been called by God to be His people, His light in the darkness of evil. We were called when we were baptized. We are being called whenever the Gospel is proclaimed to us, whether we read it or hear it or receive it in the body and blood of the Holy Sacrament. But we have a hard time answering. We hide behind the woodshed. We don't want to be the instruments by which God loves and serves His world. We don't want to do good. It is a time for ashes! A time for us to be saying, "Father, forgive us, for we don't know what we're doing." And even when we know, we can't seem to stop ourselves.

Father, forgive us!

II. The Father Forgives

Not Because of You

And, from His agony on the cross, the Christ of God who has come to take our place, our great High Priest, cries out with us in our lostness,

14

"Father, forgive them, for they know not what they do!" And the Father does forgive! The prayer of the Christ of God does not go unheard, nor does His offering on the cross go unaccepted. He forgives you! But understand it well: He does not forgive us because we somehow have deserved it. Just because you say, "I'm a sinner. I'm sorry. Forgive me," doesn't mean you have earned forgiveness. Even if you say, "I promise I'll never sin again," you still have earned nothing, deserved nothing. Besides, you wouldn't be able to keep the promise. The criminal who murders deserves no forgiveness even if he would say, "I'm sorry. I promise I won't do it again." And neither do we deserve forgiveness on any score, nor can we earn it in any way.

But Because of Jesus

We are forgiven only because it is Jesus who says, "Father, forgive them." A prisoner in jail can plead and beg and beseech, "I'm sorry. Forgive me. I promise to reform," but it will do him no good. But if the governor says, "Pardon him and let him go," he goes. So we are forgiven only because Jesus, the Christ of God, says, "Father, forgive them." That's why He came, so that we could be forgiven. The eternal Son of God was born a man of the Virgin Mary in a stable in Bethlehem so that He could say, "Father, forgive them." He lived our life, sharing our sufferings and wants and trials and temptations so that He could say, "Father, forgive them." That's why He

15

was hanging suspended there between heaven and earth on cruel and jagged spikes — so that He could say, "Father, forgive them." Without Him we are nothing but lost and rebellious sinners who don't know what we're doing. But because of Him the Father forgives.

And Now We Know What We Are Doing

The forgiveness of the Father, however, does more than wash the slate clean for us. A criminal who is pardoned is a criminal still. You can lower a fever by taking aspirin, but the infection that caused it still remains. But when the Father forgives He does more than pardon; He does more than excuse the consequences of the disease. He deals with the disease itself. He adopts us. He makes us His own. He lives in us. If sin means to walk away from God and be lost in utter confusion, not knowing what we're doing, then forgiveness is the Father reaching out to take us back to Himself. We are no longer lost, we are found. We are no longer going about in utter confusion. We are beginning to know what we are doing.

The Father who forgives us for Christ's sake is reaching out to us now as we sit in the ashes of our penitence to take us by the hand so that we might walk with Him. Not away from Him, but with Him. He is involving Himself in our life at home, on the job, in our neighborhood, and in our recreation. He is making Himself the whole point and purpose of our life. You who sit in ashes, let Him do that to you!

16

The Father who forgives us for Christ's sake is reaching out to us now as we sit in the ashes of our penitence to heal the hurts we have caused ourselves and others. He is reaching out to us who have hidden ourselves behind our fig-leaf aprons and bushes, and is making us His co-workers, His ambassadors, the body of Christ on earth. He is using us to love the world and heal it and pronounce His forgiveness to it. You who sit in ashes, let Him do that to you now!

We have come tonight to sit beneath the cross of Christ with ashes of penitence on our heads, having been rebellious, lost, and confused sinners, not knowing what we are doing. And we have heard the Christ of God above us, in the midst of His shame and agony, pray as our great High Priest, "Father, forgive them." We *are* forgiven for His sake. So let's rise from our ashes, and by the power of that forgiveness walk with the Father and every day offer ourselves to Him for Him to use.

2

The Word from the Cross:

With Me . . . in Paradise

"It's a hell of a life!" Some people say this again and again and shrug their shoulders in despair over ridding themselves of their pain and heartaches, their burdens and their trials. For many people life is hell. Hell, as we know, is to be utterly separated from God and under His holy wrath. Hell is to be abandoned by Him and forsaken by Him, forever and completely. Jesus, you remember, gives graphic illustrations of hell as "the outer darkness," as a door being shut, and hearing him say, "I never knew you. Depart from Me." Strictly speaking, hell begins for the ungodly after the Day of Judgment. But man can have a taste of hell, he can sample it for himself, while he yet lives, by abandoning God, leaving Him out of his life, and rebelling against Him. For some it is at least partially true when they say, "It's a hell of a life."

There once was a man about the same age as our Lord Jesus who felt just this way about life, only he decided that he would do something about it. He was going to get out of his hell. He was going to make his life better. But tragically he chose the way of crime and violence. It didn't help any. It only increased the torments of the hell that he made for himself. He ended up in the ancient equivalent of the electric chair — nailed to a cross and left there to die. There he hung in agony, staring into the final abyss of utter hell, and there was no escape for him. There was nothing he could do about it. Nothing! Nothing at all! The Gospel of Luke tells us what happened:

One of the criminals who were hanged railed at Him, saying, "Are you not the Christ? Save yourself and us!" But the other rebuked him, saying, "Do you not fear God, since you are under the same sentence of condemnation? And we indeed justly; for we are receiving the due reward of our deeds; but this man has done nothing wrong." And he said, "Jesus, remember me when You come in Your kingly power." And He said to him, "Truly, I say to you, today you will be with Me in Paradise." LUKE 23:39-43

So you see, this robber, facing hell, gave himself to Jesus. And our Lord took that twisted, crooked "con" with Him to Paradise. We have to do the same thing. We face our hell and then let Jesus take us with Him to Paradise.

I. Face Your Hell

We Make It Ourselves

We have to face hell, first of all. Like this criminal we too can become so hardhearted to the influence of God's Spirit that we begin to taste what it's like to be without God. For us too it can be a "hell of a life." Like the criminal we may also set out to make our life better but like him only succeed in making it worse. To be sure, we don't choose the way of crime and violence that this man walked. But we choose other ways that are equally futile. Some of us try to end the "hell" of our life by way of a better education or by getting a better job, making more money, enjoying the finer things of life, or by having fun and pleasure. We concentrate on the world and the things of the world and in the process walk even farther away from the Father. Instead of eliminating the "hell" of our life, we only succeed in making it worse.

Sometimes we try to make life better by becoming "king of the hill." Children frequently play this game. They try to get to the top and stay there, preventing anybody else from taking their place. So we think if only we could be king of the hill, then we'd escape the "hell" of our lives. If only we could be a "big shot," if only we could have power and influence and could push others around, then life would be pleasant and good. So we start pushing — our families, our neighbors, anybody who gets in the way. But instead of making life any better, we simply increase the "hell" as we fight and hurt and crush one another.

Or maybe we try to get out of our private preview of hell by trying to make ourselves worthwhile. We're going to be good and fine and noble, and everybody is going to like us. But when we concentrate on ourselves, we find only failure and inadequacy and guilt — and we've made our "hell" all the worse.

We make our own preliminary hell, you see. Real hell is to be without God, cut off from His presence, cut off from the influence of His Spirit, and spending eternity under His complete and final wrath. And we start sampling this for ourselves when in rebellion and disobedience and unfaith, we cut ourselves off from God. The robber thought he'd make things better, but he succeeded only in making his own "hell" worse. And so can we!

Face It!

The robber, as he writhed in agony on the cross, suddenly realized that he was staring straight into the abyss of hell. He had tasted hell before in his life, but now he was facing the real thing as he prepared to die. He tried to look away at first. He tried laughing at the wisecracks of the other robber who was saying, "Hey, this hurts! You're the Son of God. Why don't you get down from the cross and take us with you? Ha, ha, ha!" But now it was past the time for wisecracks, past the time for gallows humor. He was wavering in agony on the edge of the pit of death. He was facing hell itself.

I ask you to face it too. It took the cross to wake up the robber, to force him to face hell. Maybe for you it's a sudden serious illness that makes you stare suddenly into the very face of death. Or maybe it is the death of a loved one, and suddenly you're saying, "Maybe I'm next." Or maybe it's losing your job and your age makes it difficult for you to find another. Maybe it's the children growing up and leaving home and leaving you there alone. Or maybe it's finding a new wrinkle or a gray hair or seeing your bald spot in the mirror and realizing it's bigger than the last time you looked. Maybe you're suddenly left alone and you begin to ask yourself, "Why? Why am I? What is life all about? Where am I going? Why do I have to die?" In one way or the other we are forced to face the fact of death. We stare right into the abyss itself. And it is good that we do so.

Recognize that There Is No Way Out

There was no way out for the robber. He could not make a paradise out of his "hell" no matter what he did — either in a life of crime or while hanging in agony on that cross. We sometimes stare into death with a similar kind of hopelessness. No matter how hard we seek pleasure or power or prestige or popularity, no matter how desperately we cling to our youth, if we have left God the hell is still there: the "hell" of loneliness; the "hell" of war — be it with your wife or your children or your parents or your neighbor or your boss — the "hell" of hurting and being hurt; the "hell" of failure; the "hell" of emptiness in success; the "hell" of sickness and pain; and the prospect of the utter hell of death and final complete abandonment by God. And there is no way out.

II. And Go with Jesus

He Came to Get You out of Hell

The robber did the only thing he could do. He turned his head to the Man on that middle cross and, trying to focus his pain-fogged eyes, said, "Lord, remember me." Remember him for what? Remember him for how good and noble he was and for all the fine things he did in his life? He could claim nothing like that. He just said, "Remember me. I am nothing. I can claim nothing. I deserve nothing. I can only ask You to remember me — to have mercy on me." Knowing there was nothing good in his life, nothing he could cling to, he clung to Jesus. And that's what we call repentance.

How can we ever understand how Jesus' death could help that robber? We only know that Jesus said to him, "Truly, I say to you, today you will be with Me in Paradise!" What an utterly absurd thing to say, "I am going to Paradise and I shall take you with Me!" Who of *us* could ever say on our deathbed, "I'm going to heaven, and I'm taking you with me"? It's a fantastic thing to say — but He said it!

"I'll take you with Me." And this is the Good News that we are here to proclaim to each other. Since there is no way that we can wiggle out of hell — neither the final utter hell under the wrath of God nor the preliminary hell we can make for ourselves by living without God in disobedience and unfaith — because there is no way we can get out, God Himself came to pull us out. He went into death and hell Himself, so that when that robber fell into death — or you or I fall — He is there to catch us and take us out. He takes us with Him to Paradise. And this is no fable! He said it, "You will be with Me in Paradise." And it's true!

Trust Him

The robber trusted Him and is in heaven now. But it is at this point that you have to ask yourself the question in all honesty, "Do *I* trust Him?" Do you trust Him to take you to heaven when you die? And even more pertinent: do you trust Him to take you into heaven right now while you are still living? For just as we can make a preliminary hell for ourselves by forsaking God, so God can make a preliminary heaven for us by taking us to Himself to live in the peace of faith and in the power of His Spirit, while we await His coming and the perfect Paradise. The robber's trust meant that he was giving himself to Jesus so that Jesus in His mercy could take him with Him. So also your trust, your faith, means to let Jesus have you right now and to let Him give you the foretaste of Paradise in this life and the perfect Paradise in the life to come.

So trust Jesus and let Him take you along with Him into the arms of the Father. Trust Him that you are now the sons and daughters of God, that for His sake you are loved by the Creator Himself, accepted by Him, and that you belong to Him. You count for something, you matter, because Jesus takes you with Him into the arms of the Father. That's the beginning of Paradise, right now!

Trust Jesus to take you with Him right now back out into the world, not to find fun or power or prestige, but to take you out there with Him to heal — to be lights of love in the midst of the darkness of cruelty and hate, and to be the salt that preserves the people of this world from their evil and their cruelty. Let Jesus take you with Him into the world to fulfill the mission on which He sends you. When you live your life with God as God's man and God's woman on His mission, that's the beginning of Paradise, right now!

Trust Jesus to take you with Him even to the cross, to give you the power to do as He did: give your life for your neighbor instead of trying to find your life at the expense of your neighbor. "If any man would come after Me," Jesus said, "let him deny himself and take up his cross and follow Me." When we do that, seeking to give rather than to get, seeking to serve rather than to be served, seeking always to love rather than simply to be loved, then we are beginning to live in Paradise right now.

You who have tasted hell and are staring into its final abyss, Jesus is looking at you — right now. He promises you eternal life with Him in heaven and offers to take you with Him into the beginning of Paradise right now. He offers to take you into the arms of the Father to be His children, into the world to fulfill His mission, to the giving of yourself in love to your neighbor, and finally into that eternal glory that He has waiting for you. Will you trust Him? Say to Him now, as that robber did, "Lord, remember me. You who have died for me and risen again, I trust in You! Remember me!" And He will take you with Him to Paradise.

3

The Word from the Cross:

Behold Your Son . . . Your Mother

". . . standing by the cross of Jesus were His mother . . . and the disciple whom He loved."

JOHN 19:25

Why didn't she go home? It was a ghastly, hideous, terrible thing for her to watch. There hung her son in complete humiliation and shame, suffering utter agony and dying — and there was nothing she could do about it. Such lofty ideas and noble teachings, such great hopes had been centered in this her son — and it had all come to nothing. To crucifixion! She knew He was what the angel had told her, the Christ of God, He who had come from God to save the world — and this is the way the world treated its Savior. For her it must have been shattering beyond comprehension. Why didn't she go home? And over there was John, the disciple whom Jesus loved. Why was he there, standing speechless through these desolate hours? Nine of the other disciples were cowering in fear, in their bedrooms somewhere. One, who to save his own skin had denied that he ever knew Jesus, was weeping bitter tears. One was hanging from the end of a rope, a suicide, because he had betrayed his Lord. Why was John, alone of the Twelve, standing there beneath the cross? Why didn't he go home? Why are you here? I am sure that you could name quite a few things that would be more pleasant than sitting here beneath the cross of Christ. Why don't *you* go home?

I. Because We Are Loved by Christ

Christ Was Loved by His Father and So Loves Us

Mary and John were there because they couldn't help it. The love that Man dying on the cross had given them had completely overwhelmed them. They were there because they couldn't be anywhere else but at His side and in His service. But to understand that, we had best first ask the question, "What was Jesus doing there?" He who was the Son of God, with all power in heaven and on earth, through whom all things were made, why was He there, dying in agony on a cross? Because He was loved by His Father in heaven — it's as simple as that. Because He was loved by the Father who had spoken from the heavens at the time of His baptism, "This is My beloved Son in whom I am well pleased." He was loved by His Father. But what did He do with that love? Did He just bask in it and enjoy it? Did He exploit it and make an errand boy out of His Father or a kind of cosmic butler? Did He deny that love and flee from it when it began to beckon Him to the cross? None of this! He responded to His Father's love by becoming the Father's servant, the Lamb of God, the means by which God could reach out in love to save the world for Himself. Loved by the Father, He became the instrument by which God so loved the world. Christ went to the cross because the Father was loving you through Him.

And that's why Mary and John were there at the foot of the cross. God loved them through this Jesus, and this love had drawn them there to stand mutely before Him, saying in effect, "Whatever we can do; we are at Your service."

And you my brethren, why are you here? Is it not because the eternal Father has loved you through this Man impaled on that cross, and you cannot help but be here? The Father loves us and has sent His only Son to die for us! Who in all the world can ever even begin to comprehend this? The Father loves us and has sent His only Son to die for us. What else can we do but be here at the foot of His cross? I suppose we could just relax and enjoy the love of the Father, have a nice warm "religious" feeling inside, and let it go at that. Or maybe we could try using His love, praying when we're in trouble and ignoring Him the rest of the time. Or maybe we could run as fast as our legs could carry us, mouthing glib excuses all the while, whenever He starts beckoning us to take up our cross and follow Him. But if we would do that, we would be neither loving nor letting ourselves be loved. Then we would be like a girl who enjoys being admired by her "steady," and enjoys making an errand boy out of him, but runs for the hills at the very suggestion of marriage. We cannot do that! The Father has loved us through His Christ hanging there on the cross and that love draws us to Himself. We are "married" to Him, so to speak. We are here to-

33

night at the foot of His cross because we can't be anywhere else. Mute we stand before His cross and our very presence is saying, "Whatever we can do; we are at Your service."

II. We Love as the Instruments of Christ

Jesus Puts His Love into Action Through Us

And Jesus puts us in His service.

When Jesus saw His mother, and the disciple whom He loved standing near, He said to His mother, "Woman, behold your son!" Then He said to the disciple, "Behold your mother!" And from that hour the disciple took her to his own home.

John took Jesus' mother home and there provided for her. Was John just doing a favor for Jesus? No! Much more than that! The love that Jesus had for His mother was put into action through John, the disciple whom He loved. John became the means by which Jesus' love could reach out to His mother and serve her. So with us. When you do an act of kindness or love, in your home or on the job or in your neighborhood or wherever — to the friend or to the stranger, are you just doing it as a favor? No, my brethren. For us it is ever so much more than that! When you act in kindness and love to your neighbor it is Christ who is reaching out in love through you. The hands that healed are now your hands; the tongue that spoke forgiveness and love is now your tongue; the body that bore the cross for the salvation of the world is now your body. The love of Jesus for the world is put into action through you, the disciples whom He loves.

It Is Real Love in Action

You see, my brethren, love is not what so many people would have us think it is. It is not just responding to another person's lovableness, liking the likable, and despising the despicable. That kind of love is like the moon — it has no energy or power of its own, it just reflects. Nor is love just a warm feeling inside. Love is God in action through us! Love, put into us by God, is an acting concern for the good of your neighbor. Jesus on the cross didn't just say, "I love you, Mother." He said to John, "Take care of My mother as though she were your own." Nor is it love when we say, "I love my neighbor as myself, I do unto others as I would have them do unto me," and then do nothing. The love that is put into us by God is an acting concern for the good of our neighbor.

We Act by the Power of Christ's Love

But how can we love that way? It is not enough for us to know that we are supposed to love one another; not enough to know the Golden Rule, "Do unto others as you would have them do unto you," or the second Great Commandment, "Love your neighbor as yourself," or even Christ's new commandment, "Love one another as I have

35

loved you." Commands to love will not help us any more than the command to stand up straight will help a hunchback. We are able to love only because He loves us and is using us as the instruments of His love.

Perhaps you've seen one of those little wheels in a glass globe in a store window. Delicately balanced, the wheel holds small discs that are black on one side and shiny on the other. You can scream all you want at that little wheel, commanding it to spin, but it will not budge. But if you turn a light on it the wheel spins merrily, reacting to the heat. So we spin with love not because we are commanded to do so, but because the warmth of the Father's love in Christ sets us spinning.

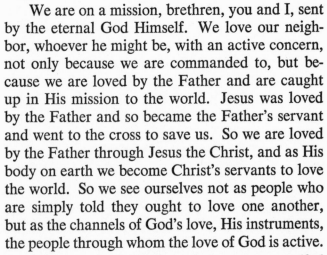

We are on a mission, brethren, you and I, sent by the eternal God Himself. We love our neighbor, whoever he might be, with an active concern, not only because we are commanded to, but because we are loved by the Father and are caught up in His mission to the world. Jesus was loved by the Father and so became the Father's servant and went to the cross to save us. So we are loved by the Father through Jesus the Christ, and as His body on earth we become Christ's servants to love the world. So we see ourselves not as people who are simply told they ought to love one another, but as the channels of God's love, His instruments, the people through whom the love of God is active.

John stood at the foot of the cross engulfed by the love with which Christ loved him. And

Jesus used him as the means by which His love could act on Mary His mother. And here you are tonight, drawn by that same love of Christ who gave Himself on the cross for you. Here and now Christ is touching you as the one by whom He will love the world. So let us leave here tonight as people who love, not because we ought to but because Jesus is acting through us. We do no one any favors; we deserve no credit; we expect no gratitude. We go forth from here tonight simply as the arms by which Christ would seek to embrace the whole world. We are the disciples whom He loves. Let His love be in action through us!

4

The Word from the Cross:

Why Hast Thou Forsaken Me?

Now from the sixth hour there was darkness over all the land until the ninth hour. And about the ninth hour Jesus cried with a loud voice, "Eli, Eli, lama sabachthani?" that is, "My God, My God, why hast Thou forsaken Me?"

MATTHEW 27:45-46

For three long hours this weird, strange, terrifying darkness hung over the land. During these long hours our Lord hung on that cross in deep agony, saying nothing, seeing nothing, but suffering everything. And then, suddenly, from the very depths of His pain and loneliness He cries out, "My God! Why hast Thou forsaken Me? Why have You left Me to suffer all this? Why must I be hanging here? Why, My God, why?" And we know a little about how He felt.

I. We Feel Forsaken

We Think We Have Been Forsaken by God

We know, because we keep asking the same question, "Why, my God, why?" Sometimes life doesn't seem to make any sense at all. The body of a fine young man with his whole life before him is brought home; he was killed in action in South Vietnam. Why, my God, why? The beautiful, the good, the loved die exhausted and spent from long battles with disease. Why, my God, why? How often don't we with all the children of men send that echoing question through the seemingly hollow halls of heaven — why, my God, why?

In the midst of the utter destruction of war,

41

when we are suffering the pains of others, when our hearts ache over our children or bleed for our husband or wife, when we hurt and we don't know the reason for it all, we have cried out, "Why, my God, why?" Even when we are in the midst of joy and happiness and everything is going well, we sense that things are hollow and empty; every party, sooner or later, has to be over. Why, my God, why? We are full of anxiety and big, undefined question marks about who we are and why we are and where we are going so rapidly, so inescapably; like astronauts on a rocket we can do absolutely nothing to stop ourselves. Why, my God, why?

We are often filled with a sense of dread, of some kind of doom hanging over us and all sorts of malevolent forces acting against us trying to hurt us. And we are afraid. We are afraid of ourselves and what we might do to mess up our lives or others' lives, afraid of each other, afraid of being alone, afraid of the future, afraid of death, and, ultimately, afraid of God. Why, my God, why? Why have You forsaken me?

But It Is We Who Have Forsaken Him

We blame it all on God. Somehow we think it's all His fault. What kind of a God is this that lets these fine young men die in South Vietnam and our loved ones die in battles with disease? If there is a God and He's a good God, then why must there be all this suffering and anxiety and fear and dread and loneliness and lovelessness and hatred and cruelty? Why do You do it to us, God? Why have You forsaken us?

But, really, it is not He who has forsaken us. It is we who have forsaken Him. The eternal God, your Creator and Redeemer, does not want you to be miserable. He has not made you to be full of anxiety and dread, full of fear and hatred and anger and loneliness. He has not even made you to die. We have forsaken Him and brought all these consequences upon ourselves.

It is as if I were on a yacht, and it is very hot. The water looks very cool and inviting and I'd like to go swimming. But the captain of the yacht warns me against swimming, "There are dangerous currents here, a lot of man-eating sharks, and besides you don't even know how to swim." But the water looks so cool and nice. So I jump in. And then in the agony of my bleeding wounds from the sharks, my lungs filling with water, I cry out in anger against the captain, "Why have you forsaken me?" He has not forsaken me. I have forsaken him!

So it is with all mankind. We have walked out on God and brought all these calamities upon ourselves and then say to God, "Why have You forsaken me?" The world and all mankind are profoundly out of joint; we know it and can see it and suffer under it — but we are helpless to do much about it. Adam and Eve, expelled from the Garden of Eden because they refused to live with their Creator, walked from perfection to the pain and suffering and wrongness of the wilderness.

What happened to them has happened to us. We're all in this together.

But if you say, "I have never forsaken God," then, my brother, you do not know yourself. What Adam and Eve did, you have done and are doing. The pain and predicament of mankind is also your pain and predicament, for you are a part of mankind. What is it that you love most dearly? What do you think is the highest good? What would you most like to have or to be? What is it that motivates your decisions, why do you do what you do? Is the answer to these questions God, the Father of our Lord Jesus Christ? Could you answer even one of them in that manner? I doubt it. We have forsaken God! Every time you break a commandment knowingly you are in danger of showing God, yourself, and the whole world that you have forsaken Him. And when you don't break a commandment but want to, you risk forsaking Him inside.

Because we have forsaken Him, life in this world is profoundly out of order. Sin brings its own punishment; it bears its own consequences. The man who drinks too much gets drunk and eventually destroys his body. The man who commits adultery destroys his home and family. And when we have forsaken God we are anxious and full of dread and fear and loneliness and anger and hate and hurt. "My God, why have You forsaken me?" we say, only because we would rather blame God than face up to the fact that it is we who have forsaken Him.

II. The Word from the Cross Shows We Are Not Forsaken

Jesus Shared Our Sinfulness

But Jesus, the Christ of God, innocent and holy, the only-begotten Son of God, why should He have screamed this agony, "My God, why have You forsaken Me?" If anyone should have known that He was not forsaken of the Father, it was Jesus. Why was the silent darkness suddenly split as by a thunderclap with this frightening lament from the Son of God, the Savior of the world? Who can say? No one can ever really comprehend what was happening there on the hill called Golgotha when the dying Prince of Life hung suspended between heaven and earth. This much we know: that He was one of us, for we heard Him shout in the darkness the same agonizing question that haunts us. This much we know: man has forsaken the Father, and Jesus of Nazareth, the Christ of God, the incarnate Son of God, bore the consequences. Adam and Eve walked out of the Garden of Eden, and Jesus walked with them into the wilderness. Mankind has jumped out of the boat, and Jesus has jumped in with us to share our suffering and save us. The whole world is out of joint, and Jesus takes on the consequences. We have forsaken God, and Jesus bears the anxiety, the fear, and the loneliness, and shouts out: "My God, why hast Thou forsaken Me?" This much we know.

45

Jesus Took the Consequences for Us

But there is more involved than that. From the perspective of the open tomb, knowing that Jesus has risen from the dead, this we also believe: Jesus not only shared the consequences *with* us, He bore the consequences *for* us. It is as though Jesus walked out of the Garden of Eden with Adam and Eve and said, "You stay here. I'll walk alone through the dry and blasted places of the wilderness, forsaken by God, so that you can go back into the Garden of Eden, back to Paradise." It is as though He jumped out of the yacht and gave Himself to the sharks while boosting us back into the safety of the ship. We forsake the Father in heaven and are forsaking Him still, but it is Jesus who takes the punishment for us. It is in your place and in your stead that Jesus suffered the hell of abandonment by God and shouted out, "My God, my God, why hast Thou forsaken Me?" I do not pretend to understand all this, but I proclaim to you what has been proclaimed for nearly 2,000 years, the good news of God, the good word from the cross: Christ was forsaken by God *instead of you*. He took the consequences so you don't have to suffer them.

From This We Know that He Has Not Forsaken Us

So brethren, go back to Eden, go back to Paradise, go back into the boat. God has *not* forsaken you! The cross shouts it out to us loud and clear: the Father has not forsaken us! When you feel anxious and full of dread about who you are and why you are living and where you are going, the cross of Christ is your Rock and Fortress, and you can shout, "My God, my Father, You have not forsaken me!" When you are suffering pain or heartache or loneliness, then the cross of Christ is your Rock and Fortress, and you can shout, "My God, my Father, You have not forsaken me!" When you are angry and full of hate and evil and feeling guilty as though in hell itself, then the cross of Christ is your Rock and Fortress, and you can shout, "My God, my Father, You have not forsaken me!" When you are facing death and the eternal Judge, then the cross of Christ is your Rock and Fortress, and you can shout, "My God, my Father, You have not forsaken me!"

This I ask of you: hear Jesus crying out in darkness and in hell, "My God, My God, why hast Thou forsaken Me?" Hear, and know that He shares with you the consequences of your sin and rebellion. Hear it and know that He suffered all the consequences of your sin and rebellion *for* you. From now on, whenever you are suffering pain or heartache or fear or loneliness or whatever, and you are tempted to cry out, "Why, God, why have You forsaken me?" look to the cross instead and hear the forsaken voice of the Christ of God who saved you. Say instead, "My God, my Father, You have not forsaken me!"

5

The Word from the Cross:

I Thirst

> After this Jesus, knowing that all was now finished, said (to fulfill the Scripture), "I thirst." A bowl full of vinegar stood there; so they put a sponge full of the vinegar on hyssop and held it to His mouth.
>
> JOHN 19:28-29

For many long hours Jesus had hung there on that cross, suffering all the tortures of crucifixion and all the agonies of hell itself. When they nailed Him there He had refused the drink of wine that had been mixed with myrrh, a kind of primitive pain-killer. But now, with His lips cracked and His throat dry as dust, He can stand it no longer. From the cross there comes this hoarse word of human suffering, "I thirst." And we hear it! We are gathered here tonight at the foot of His cross and we hear that cracking cry of pain. What shall we do about it? Some of the people who stood under that cross merely shook their heads in pity and walked away. Some of the calloused bystanders laughed and said, "Let's see if Elijah will come and help Him." And one soldier gave Him a drink — a drink of vinegar. But what will we do? We are here tonight to listen to that groan again — and to find in the power of His love the ability to give Him a drink.

I. He Is Thirsty

He Shares Our Thirst

Our Lord is thirsty. But the thirst of the Christ of God involves more than just a dry throat

51

that hasn't had any liquid for many hours and is now racked with fever. For this Jesus is the One whom God has appointed to take the place of all mankind. He is my substitute, and yours, and every man's, going all the way back to Adam and Eve. Jesus is the summation of the whole human race. He is all of mankind in one Person. So when He moans in agony on that cross, "I thirst," He is giving voice to all humanity's yearning for drink, for wholeness. We are all thirsty — and it is His swollen tongue that must say the thick words, "I thirst." We are all thirsty because we have all turned away from the only water that can satisfy our thirst, the Water of Life that comes from God Himself. Whenever (and we do this all the time) we declare our independence from God saying, "Please, God, I'd rather do it myself"; whenever we leave God out of our lives and out of our decisions; whenever we decide to choose for ourselves what to do with our lives; whenever we decide for ourselves what is right and what is wrong, then we are walking away from the Fountain of Life into the desert where no water is. Turned in upon ourselves we do not give any drink to the thirsty or receive any from their hands. And it is Jesus' throat that voices every man's agonizing need, "I thirst."

We Thirst for Each Other

For what, then, do we thirst? Surely we can see that it is for more than water. Our cry of thirst is like the Psalmist who says, "O God . . . my

52

God . . . my soul thirsts for Thee . . . as in a dry and weary land where no water is." (Ps. 63:1) We thirst for God. We thirst for that wholeness and peace and understanding that only belonging to God can give us. We thirst for love. We thirst for forgiveness, for acceptance, and for understanding. We thirst for help in our troubles, for healing of our wounds and our heartaches. But just as Christ's aching thirst was satisfied by a fellow human being squeezing a sponge full of vinegar in His face, so our thirst for God is to be satisfied through our brother. I thirst for God's love and forgiveness and acceptance, but that thirst is best satisfied only when you love me and forgive me and accept me in God's name. I thirst for understanding, for help and for healing, but God satisfies that thirst when you understand and help and seek to give me healing in God's name. For what do we thirst? We thirst for God. We thirst for God to be with us and to help us through our brother — through each other.

We Thirst to Give Ourselves to Each Other

But far more profoundly, we thirst not just for God to help us through our brother, but we thirst for God to help our brother through us. Our need is not just to receive a drink. We also have the need to be the kind of people who give a drink to those who are thirsty. We have a need to be servants. And that really is a very disquieting thing to say. When we serve someone, we usually do it as a favor, or out of a sense of duty, or as

53

an unpleasant chore that simply needs to be done. But that is all wrong. Rather, if we want to be whole and happy people we need to be people who serve. Look at your Lord Jesus. He was God's perfect Son, the way a man really ought to be, and He lived the way a man really ought to live. He is the perfect example of what it means to be alive, to be a human being. And this Jesus was a man who lived for others, not for Himself! He told us, "I am among you as One who serves." (Luke 22:27) He was "a man for others." To be a man who exists only for himself is to be utterly alone. Life is then all twisted, and we become miserable, full of hates and angers and jealousies and hurts. But to be a man who lives to serve other people in God's name is to be like Jesus, to have a taste of heaven, to be fulfilled and happy. Our greatest thirst then, you see, is not just to be loved and served by God through our brother, but to love and serve our brother in God's name. Our greatest thirst is not for a drink, but to give a drink to the thirsty.

II. Give Him a Drink

His Thirst Confronts Us in Our Brother

Your Lord is thirsty, my brethren. Give Him a drink! The soldiers heard His dry, cracked voice sounding from the cross above them. You hear it somewhere else. You hear Him in every pleading voice or in every hungry eye that comes

54

your way day by day. Jesus Himself said, "As you did it to one of the least of these My brethren, you did it to Me" (Matt. 25:40). Jesus confronts us in the thirsty need of our neighbor, every neighbor whose path we cross. The wife who wants her husband to love her and be good to her is Christ saying, "I thirst." The husband who wants his wife to respect him and help him is Christ saying, "I thirst." The neighbor who has trouble with her children, the man on the job who has trouble with drinking, the fellow student who is lonely and unpopular, the frustrated slum-dweller who has lost all hope, the citizen of Vietnam whose family has been killed or maimed and whose house and farm is utterly lost, and so on and on — each of these is Christ saying to you, "I thirst." Listen to Him! Don't just shake your head in pity and walk away. Don't just laugh and say, "Maybe Elijah will help — or some government welfare agency." Listen to Him, and give Him a drink!

But Don't Give Him Vinegar

But don't give Him vinegar! That was a sour wine that the soldiers had around, the cheapest drink available. Your thirsty Lord deserves more from you than that! But often that's all that we offer Him. Suppose your neighbor is in need and you offer him help grudgingly, because you can't get out of it — that's cheap vinegar. Or if your neighbor is in need and you help him only out of a sense of duty, because you feel you must — that's sour wine. Or if your only motive in helping the needy is so that they'll stop being a burden on the taxpayer — that's cheap vinegar. And it's pretty sour wine, too, if you only help from a distance, like giving money to a charity or giving money to missions, but not helping the needy personally or speaking the Gospel person to person. We can do better than that!

Be Moved by His Love

Give Him a drink in response to His love for you. No other drink can satisfy His thirst, or your need to give it. Look at that soldier who gave Christ the drink. Some shook their heads in pity and walked away. Others laughed and waited for Elijah to help Him. But one of them gave Him a drink. Why? Maybe it was only out of pity, and maybe he jammed it roughly into our Lord's face with a mocking laugh. Maybe. But maybe he was brought to that act of kindness by the love that reached out even to him from that cross. Let us hope so! But in any case that is the only power anywhere that can enable us to be people who serve Christ in their neighbor. Pity won't do it. A sense of duty won't help much. Enlightened self-interest is only sour wine. But the love of the Father is reaching out to us through the sacrifice of His Son on the altar of the cross. The love of the Father is touching us in the Word and in the Sacrament. This love can transform us into new creations who are able to serve Christ in our neighbor. We are loved by the Father! We are forgiven our sins by His precious blood, His innocent suffering and death. We are accepted by the Father into that vast, marching company of His men and women who know what it means to be alive, who know what it means to be human, who know what it means to be happy and useful, who know what it means to be Christians — Christ's men and women. The power of that love that brought His Christ to the cross for us is the power that enables us to give Him a drink in the unselfish joy of service.

That love is touching you now. And all around you from myriads of suffering throats you hear the voice of your Savior, "I thirst." Give Him a drink!

6

The Word from the Cross:

It Is Finished

When Jesus had received the vinegar, He said, "It is finished." JOHN 19:30

As you listen to your Savior speaking through the fog of His agony the word, "It is finished," look at Him closely. That is not the face of one dejected and in despair as the end draws near. Look closely and see that He is not referring to the fact that His agony is now ending, that the malice and the hatred and the pain which broke His heart are now done and set aside forever. Nor is He merely saluting death and saying good-bye to life as so many brave men have done before and since Good Friday. Look closely. That face, bloody and contorted, is yet bright and at peace. These are not the words of a man who is surrendering to death, but the words of a soldier who has conquered in the battle, the words of a Savior whose work has been accomplished, the words of a builder whose job is done.

I. Christ Has Finished His Work

As a Soldier

A soldier who returns from a climactic battle in which he has been victorious may be very weary and battle-scarred, but he will not be dejected and despairing when he says, "It is finished!" Rather there will be joy and triumph in his voice because of his victory. So also our Lord Jesus, hanging in agony on that cross, is a soldier home from a climactic battle. Who can imagine, much less speak

61

of, the battle that raged in those hours of darkness around the cross? Who can even begin to comprehend what happened when the Son of God fought with Satan for the souls of the whole world? Look again at that soldier on the cross. He may indeed be weary and bloody, but He is not dejected and despairing when He says, "It is finished!" This is triumph! He has won the war!

As a Savior

Or think of it this way. A lifeguard on the beach who wades ashore with a child in his arms that he has just rescued from drowning may be exhausted and gasping for breath, but he will not be dejected and despairing when he says, "It is finished." There will be joy and triumph in his voice because he has saved a child from drowning. So also the Lord Christ, hanging in agony on that cross, is a Savior, one who has just rescued the whole world from drowning in the buffeting and battering, crashing waves of life. Look at Him again on that cross. He may be exhausted and gasping for breath, but He is not dejected and despairing when He says, "It is finished!" Everything necessary for our salvation has been accomplished. This is triumph! He has saved the whole world!

As a Builder

Or look at it this way. A builder who has just finished building a home for his bride may be tired and dirty from the job, but he will not be dejected and despairing when he says to his bride, "It is finished!" Rather there will be happiness and joy and an eager expectation in his voice as he looks for the happiness that will light up his bride's eyes when he shows her their new home. So Christ, hanging in agony on that cross, has just finished building a mansion in heaven for His bride, the church. Look at Him again there on that cross. He may be tired. He may be dirty from the shameful, degrading treatment the sons of men have given Him, the Son of God, but He is not dejected and despairing when He says, "It is finished!" This is triumph! He has built for us an eternal home!

II. Is It Finished for You?

Or Are You Still in Bondage?

It is finished. He has done His work. But now we must ask the question, "Is it finished for you?" Is it really finished for you or are you still in bondage to that which makes life ugly and painful and evil? You don't have to live in slavery to all that anymore. You don't have to live in evil. You don't have to jettison goodness and kindness and love from your life in order to get ahead in your job or in society, making yourself miserable and continually hurting others in the process. You don't have to live with a sense of guilt and failure and despair. Don't you see Him on the cross, the victorious soldier home from the

63

battle? Listen to Him saying, "It is finished!" That means you are forgiven, freely and fully.

Since Christ has died for your sins, God holds nothing against you, for Christ's sake. So why should you hold anything against yourself and go around feeling guilty and evil? Or why should you make your life miserable trying to prove to yourself and to God that you really are good, never quite believing it yourself? You don't have to prove anything anymore. You don't have to earn approval from God. You don't have to merit His love. It is finished! You are forgiven — freely and fully. God loves you as you are, no matter what you are or what you have done, for Christ's sake. This is an awesome thing to say! It makes your heart sing with joy and wonder. He loves you — as you are, and accepts you — as you are, for Christ's sake. So why shouldn't you now love yourself as God loves you, and see yourself as a man or a woman who is lovely and accepted and worthwhile because of Jesus Christ?

Take, for example, a young lady who is quite homely. As she grows older she begins to despair and to dislike herself. She feels that no one could possibly love her, much less marry her. But then the right man comes along, who sees her real beauty and loves her and marries her. Then she is absolutely transformed! She sees herself as a person who is lovely and worthwhile, for she sees herself through her husband's eyes, and all life blooms for her.

So God loves you and has married you. It is

finished! Now you can look at yourself through the eyes of your Lord Jesus. You can see yourself as someone lovely and acceptable and worthwhile, and all life blooms for you because of Jesus Christ. Through Christ's victory you have power to be a saint of God. Will you not take that power and live in the joy of being one of God's own, happy people? It is finished! Is it finished for you?

Or Are You Still Drowning?

Or are you still drowning, buffeted by the waves of tragedy and heartache, or sinking into the quicksand of success and luxury, getting so concerned about things that you forget about God? It doesn't have to be that way anymore! You don't have to be afraid of anything. You don't have to be afraid of the bomb. You don't have to be afraid for your job or your family. You don't have to be so absorbed in material things that you lose your own soul. You need not fear Judgment Day. Look at Jesus on the cross. There is the Savior who is holding you in His arms, saying, "It is finished. I have saved you. You belong to Me." He has taken the sting from the buffeting and crashing waves and from the heartaches, pains, and troubles of your life. Only now put yourself into those arms and relax. There is much more to life than success and possessions. There is so much joy in living with God that no heartache or pain or loss can ever take it away from you. You belong to the Father. You are His forever and ever. He has saved you and you belong to Him. It is finished! Is it finished for you?

Or Are You Still Lonely, Afraid, and Lost?

Or are you still going through life lonely and afraid and lost? Do you still feel like that little 2-year-old Korean child in that famous picture taken during the Korean War? There sat that little child in the ruins of a railway station, injured and bleeding, ragged, his parents dead, afraid, alone, completely lost and crying in his terror. Do you still feel like that? Do you still feel like a "thought, a homeless thought, wandering forlorn through the empty centuries," as Mark Twain once put it? You don't have to feel that way anymore. You don't have to be lonely. Take His hand — He's holding it out to you. You don't have to be lost — He'll lead you home. You don't have to be afraid — He'll take you through the valley of the shadow of death into the Father's house. Has He not said, "In My Father's house are many rooms . . . I go to prepare a place for you"? Look at Him on that cross. There is the Master Builder with a smile on His face, saying to his bride, "It is finished!" He wants to show you the home that He has built for you. Take Him by the hand and be no longer lonely and lost and afraid. It is finished. You are going home!

Look at the Christ of God very carefully on that cross as He says, "It is finished." There is the soldier home victorious from the battle against sin and evil. There is the Savior who has rescued you from all the buffeting waves of the sea of life. There is the builder who has built you an eternal home. It is finished! Let it now be finished for you! As His head begins to sink in death, let your head rise up with joy and peace and security. It is finished!

7

The Word from the Upper Room:

A New Covenant

MAUNDY THURSDAY

> This is My blood of the covenant, which is poured
> out for many for the forgiveness of sins.
>
> MATTHEW 26:28

Look around. Here we are, gathered at this altar, celebrating the anniversary of our Lord's institution of the Holy Eucharist. On this night we are all here with one purpose: to eat a piece of bread and drink a sip of wine — with elaborate ritual and much devotion.

Why do we do it? The answer we would all give is very simple: to receive the forgiveness of sins. We believe and confess that we receive "in, with, and under" the bread and wine the true body and blood of our Lord Jesus Christ, given and shed for us for the forgiveness of sins. But the problem is that we often have a far too narrow understanding of what the forgiveness of sins is. We may have a picture of God up in heaven with a big, black book in His hands in which our names are recorded. Every time we sin, a black mark is struck behind our name. Then, when we go to Holy Communion, all the black marks are erased and the holy angel soon starts entering the black marks all over again. As a result of this we have such strange distortions as some people thinking: "I won't go to Holy Communion too often. I'll let those black marks pile up awhile so that going to Holy Communion will really be worthwhile." Or they think: "I had better not go to Holy Communion too often or people will suppose I am a terrible sinner who needs lots of forgiveness."

How sad if we feel that way! Sin, repentance,

and forgiveness are much more than a matter of celestial bookkeeping. Sin disrupts man's fellowship with God; it is rebellion, separation, a running away from home like the prodigal son. The black marks recording the evil that we do and the good we fail to do are the symptoms of the disruption of that fellowship with God. Because of that disruption God seems to be the condemning Judge rather than the loving and waiting Father. Forgiveness of sins means much more than erasing black marks from a book. Forgiveness means a restoration of the fellowship, a coming home of the penitent to the waiting arms of the Father.

Listen again to what Jesus said as He passed the cup on this night, "This is My blood *of the covenant,* which is poured out for many for the forgiveness of sins." The blood of the covenant! Or as St. Paul quotes Jesus in the Epistle, "This cup is the new *covenant* in My blood." So you see that when we talk about the forgiveness of sins here, we do not just mean erasing black marks. We mean the forgiveness of sins that renews a covenant with God.

What is a covenant? It is a relationship between two parties, a contract, an agreement. Simply stated, the covenant or relationship which God has established with His people is this: God says, "I shall be your God and you shall be My people. We shall be together. We shall have fellowship. We shall be Father and son. Nothing will separate us — not even your sin, for I forgive it." God makes this covenant unilaterally, with no ifs, ands,

72

or buts, with no strings attached. Now in response to this Good News His people reply, "Yes! You shall be our God and we shall be Your people. We believe your promise. We want Your forgiveness and penitently we come to receive it. We want Your Spirit so that we can not only be but also behave as Your people."

God is very much concerned about this relationship between Himself and us. So He gives to us the forgiveness of sins so that the relationship of Father and son might be restored and be real, living, and functioning. "This is My blood of the covenant," Jesus says. Let us look from this angle at what Jesus did this night, and at what is happening every time we celebrate the Holy Eucharist.

I. God Says, "I Am Yours"

He Gives Us Christ

We are here tonight — and every time we come to this altar — to hear God say to us, "I am yours! I am your God, I give Myself to you." This is really the content of our faith, isn't it? This is the whole message of the Gospel, God gives Himself to us in Christ so that He might be our Father. And this is such an awesome thing to say! The great and holy God, hidden in His majesty and glory, beyond all human understanding, so holy that no man can see Him and live, this God gives Himself to us to be our Father — to us, the rebels who have run away, the weak, the evil,

73

the sinners, the uncaring. It is really overwhelming! But it is true. God gives Himself to us to be our Father. That is why He sent His Christ, the Son of God, who was conceived by the Holy Ghost, born of the Virgin Mary and was made man. Indeed, God gave Himself to us all the way to the cross. God-made-man dies for us in our place as He pays for our sin on that cross, so that He might be our God and we might be His people. Before you stands the cross, and from it the eternal holy God is saying His good word to us, "See, I am yours, I give Myself to you. I am your God and you are My people."

And He Gives Us the Sacrament

And that's what He says and does in the Holy Sacrament we are celebrating. In a mystery beyond explanation or understanding God here gives Himself to us so that He might be our Father in the true body and blood of our Lord Jesus Christ that was given and shed for us on Calvary for the forgiveness of sins. The Son of God came to the world to save it, to bring it back into covenant with God by the forgiveness of sins. Now here Jesus comes to *you* to bring that salvation to you personally, to bring you back into covenant with God. As we eat the body and drink the blood of Christ, God is saying to us, "I am your God. I give Myself to *you*." So we eat and drink not only to receive assurance that the black marks are indeed erased, but to enter into covenant with God as He gives Himself to us. The eternal God made

74

Himself our Father by giving us His Son to be our Savior. Now He gives to us the assurance that in Christ He is our Father, and we are forgiven as we eat and drink the body and blood given and shed for us.

II. We Say, "We Are Yours"

We Trust His Forgiveness

But as God gives Himself to us in Jesus Christ and makes a covenant with us saying, "See, I am yours," so we are moved to reply, "Yes, You are our God — and we are Your people." And this is what *we* are doing here tonight as we eat and drink this body and blood of our Lord Jesus Christ. We are here because we believe God when He says to us in Jesus Christ, "I am yours!" We are here because we believe that Jesus of Nazareth, crucified under Pontius Pilate, was God-made-man, and that His death has brought us forgiveness and restored us to a covenant with God. So when we kneel here at the rail to receive Christ we are saying "yes" to God's covenant. We are saying, "I am sorry for my sins. I believe and I trust that Christ's death on the cross gives me forgiveness of sins and brings me back to God." God, so to speak, reaches down to us through Christ and through the Sacrament and says, "I forgive you; I am yours." We kneel here in faith and receive Christ in the bread and wine and say, "I believe You." We reach out our hands

to His and say, "We are Yours." So our hands
meet, and the covenant in His blood is renewed
again.

We Offer Ourselves

But to take His hand in faith and to renew the
covenant implies more than our saying, "I believe
I am forgiven — the black marks are erased."
To accept that covenant saying, "You are our God
and we are Your people," is to offer ourselves to
Him. This is why Luther could say that the only
sacrifice of the mass is the sacrifice of ourselves.
To kneel here and receive the body and blood of
Christ is as it were to place yourself on the altar,
to offer up yourself as a living sacrifice to God for
Him to use as He sees fit. This is part of the covenant. As you receive His body and blood and so
enter into covenant with Him, you are saying,
"Take me and use me. Let me be Your man,
Your woman, a part of Your body, the instrument
by which You carry out Your saving and loving
work in the world." In this way we enter into the
covenant He has made with us.

On this night Jesus spoke this good word to us,
"This is My blood of the covenant" — or, as Saint
Paul quotes Him, "This cup is the new covenant
in My blood." You see then what forgiveness of
sins includes. It is God giving Himself to us in
Jesus Christ through His Sacrament and saying,
"I am yours. I am your Father." Now it is for us
to kneel here and receive Christ and say, "Yes,
I believe You. You are my God who forgives me,

my Father who loves me. Now I give myself to You. I am Yours to use." Where there is forgiveness, the covenant is renewed.

Our Lord is here tonight saying, "I am yours. I give Myself to you. I make a covenant with you." So now come, and enter into that covenant saying, "Yes. I am Yours. I give myself to You."

8

The Word from the Cross:

Father, into Thy Hands
I Commit My Spirit

GOOD FRIDAY

Then Jesus, crying with a loud voice, said, "Father, into Thy hands I commit My spirit!" And having said this He breathed His last.   LUKE 23:46

Late this afternoon, death finally came to our Lord as He hung there in agony, nailed to the cross. Death claimed the living God who was Himself the Prince of Life, and around the world birds sang, millions of people laughed and cried, and business went on as usual. Of all the millions of people in the world, who knew what was happening on this little hill called Golgotha in a despised country off in a corner of the world? And of those who knew, who really cared? Death came to the One who had come to give life — and only a handful knew or cared.

Today, on this anniversary of His death, the sun still shines and birds still sing, people still laugh and cry, and business still goes on as usual. Of all the billions of people in this world, who knows what happened on this day, and knowing, cares? But we know, and we care, for in this moment when death claimed Jesus of Nazareth our lives were radically changed. In this seventh word from the cross Christ gives His life to God, and with this offering our lives, too, are given to God!

I. Christ Gives His Life to God

In Perfect Trust

"Father, into Thy hands I commit My spirit," He said. "Father, into Your hands I am placing

My life." Here is the true, the perfect man giving us an example of complete trust in God. But a short time before this Christ was crying out in the agony of hell itself, "My God, My God, why hast Thou forsaken Me?" He was forsaken as we shall never be forsaken. Yet, even in this He did not rebel against His Father, nor rail in anger toward Him. With the perfect confidence of one who knew His Father's love and care He placed His life into His Father's hands, without a murmur or a question or a doubt. This is what we mean when we sing in our hymn, "Learn of Jesus Christ to die."

The Perfect Sacrifice

But in this seventh word of our Savior we can see more than confident trust. In this moment, as He places His life into the hands of God and dies, He is giving to God the perfect sacrifice, offered in payment for the sins of the world. He is a Lamb "without blemish and without spot." His was the perfect life, a life that knew and endured all that mankind endures, that knew temptation in every respect as we do, yet never fell into any sin. "Father, into Thy hands I commit My spirit," Jesus said. "Father, I place into Your hands My perfect life. Let it count for the perfection of all men." It was the ultimate sacrifice, the only sacrifice that could possibly pay for man's guilt. How could the sacrifice of animals ever remove the stain of our guilt before the holy God? (They could only point to Christ's sacrifice.) Or how could man's feeble attempts at goodness make us right with God when God's holiness demands perfect obedience? But here was the death of the infinite God-made-man! It is mysterious, unthinkable, incomprehensible! Yet here on the cross it is taking place. "Father, into Thy hands I commit My spirit," Jesus said. "Father, I place into Your hands the perfect sacrifice. Let it pay for the sins of the world." And on the third day, God spoke His *yes!*

II. So Now Give Your Life to God

We Also Are Offered to God

This transforms our whole life! This was the perfect life which counts now for our perfection, the perfect sacrifice which pays for all the evil that we are and do. It is the purchase of our forgiveness, our holiness, that is placed into the hands of God. Indeed, it is we ourselves who are here placed into the Father's hands. When Christ gave His life to God, we, who by Baptism and faith are united to Christ, were also given to God as redeemed, purchased, and forgiven people. "Father, into Thy hands I commit My spirit," Jesus said. "Here is My life, Father, the perfect sacrifice, and here are the lives of all those who by faith have received the benefits of this sacrifice through Baptism and participation in My body and blood given and shed for the forgiveness of sins."

Given to God, We Live for God

What a transformation this works in our lives! It makes us a whole new creation! Having been given to God, we live with God. Too often we treat the business of living in the world and living with God as though they were far apart and mutually exclusive. Because we do that, it is not surprising that God seems far away and unimportant. He is too often regarded as simply a possible help in trouble but otherwise irrelevant. The result is that we are in danger of living in the emptiness and futility of a phony religion. But when Christ gave His life to God, He gave you to God also. The Father is not distant and far away! You have been given to the Father! You are with Him, and He is with you. So our Christianity is not just a matter of religious duties halfheartedly fulfilled. It is a life lived with God. Our Christian faith is not like an eternal-life-insurance policy, it is life with God right now! Hear His cry in the agony of death, "Father, into Thy hands I commit My spirit," and know that you also are given to God in this dying breath. Know it. Believe it. And live it! Your life has been changed!

Having Been Given to God, Live with That Point of View

Your life has also been changed in this that you now see life from your heavenly Father's point of view. Everything in life depends upon your point of view. To a farmer crying to God for rain

84

to save his crops a thunderstorm is a blessing. To a child expecting to go on a picnic that day the same storm is a terrifying tragedy. When we look at the world from the point of view of those who are not with the Father, life can look most tragic. The fears, the dangers, the uncertainties, the heartaches, the tragedies, death, seem enormous and crushing, like a mountain viewed from the plain. But get a different point of view, fly above a mountain, and it seems flattened out and rather harmless. You have a new point of view. When Christ gave His life to God He gave Him yours, too. Your life is now "hid with Christ in God." You are His own, "the people of His pasture, and the sheep of His hand." From this point of view all the fears, dangers, uncertainties, heartaches, tragedies, and death are flattened out. Life is robbed of its terrors and we live in confidence and peace with the Father who has promised He will make everything in life work out for our good.

Having Been Given to God, Trust Him in the Hour of Death

Even death is changed for us! Because Christ has placed our lives into the hands of the Father as He placed His own life there, we can echo His trust and confidence in the hour of our death. "Father, into Thy hands I commit My spirit," Jesus said, and died in perfect peace and with calm trust in His Father. We can do that, too. Whether death comes tonight or tomorrow, suddenly or in agonizing slowness, we can say,

"Father, into Thy hands I commit my spirit." We can say that because Christ has placed our lives into the Father's hand, and not even death can take us from Him.

"Father, into Thy hands I give My life," Christ said, and in doing this He gave to God the perfect sacrifice that made us His. Indeed, He gave us to the Father, too. This has changed our life! So live for God! Live with the Father's point of view! Trust Him with perfect peace in the hour of death!

The Christ of God died while birds sang, millions of people laughed and cried, and business went on as usual. Who knows? Or knowing, cares? We do! Because our lives have been given to God!

9

The Word from the
Empty Tomb:

We Are Risen!

THE FEAST OF THE RESURRECTION

Do you not know that all of us who have been baptized into Christ Jesus were baptized into His death? We were buried therefore with Him by Baptism into death, so that as Christ was raised from the dead by the glory of the Father, we too might walk in newness of life. For if we have been united with Him in a death like His, we shall certainly be united with Him in a resurrection like His. We know that our old self was crucified with Him so that the sinful body might be destroyed, and we might no longer be enslaved to sin. For he who has died is freed from sin. But if we have died with Christ, we believe that we shall also live with Him. For we know that Christ, being raised from the dead, will never die again; death no longer has dominion over Him. The death He died He died to sin, once for all, but the life He lives He lives to God. So you also must consider yourselves dead to sin and alive to God in Christ Jesus. ROMANS 6:3-11

How wonderful it is to be alive! When it's springtime and the sun is shining and the robins are singing and everything is going well for you, your heart can be bursting with joy. It's great to be alive! It's a shame that feeling doesn't last. The cold winds blow and it gets all gloomy and rainy, the boss chides you at work, your husband or wife is grouchy as a bear, the children get sick and you catch the flu, and then who says it's great to be alive? But don't you think the joy of living ought to depend on something more substantial than the state of the weather or your husband's disposition or the workings of your digestive system? It *is* great to be alive! There is a wonder and a joy to life that is far beyond the joy of spring and a healthy body. That is the great Good News we are here to proclaim to one another today. Jesus is alive! He is risen from the dead! And that means *we* are risen from the dead! We too are alive! Really alive! And it's great!

To say that Jesus rose from the dead is an interesting fact of history about which people can speculate. Some will deny it ever happened, some will try to explain it, and some will try to prove it. Well, it *is* a fact of history, that's true, and it is the very foundation of our faith, proving to us that Jesus of Nazareth is what we proclaim Him to be, the Son of God and the Savior of the world, not a tragic martyr or a self-deluded fraud. But our proclamation to one another and to the world this morning is more than the telling of a fact of history. We are proclaiming not only that Jesus rose from the dead, but that He rose from the dead *for you!* To say that Jesus rose from the dead is like handling an electric cord. To say that He rose *for you* is to plug that wire into an electric socket. When you handle that wire now, something happens! There is power there now! Power to kill, as when wire is connected to an electric chair. Power to give life, as when wire is used to shock a heart that has stopped beating into pulsating life once again. And that's what the proclamation of Easter is to do to us today, kill us — make us dead to sin — and make us alive — fill us with such genuine joy that we can walk away from here today, facing ill health, sour bosses, grouchy husbands or wives, rainy weather, and everything else and say, "It's great to be alive!"

I. We Have Died with Christ

When He Died, We Died

The life that is great is a resurrected life. And if there is going to be resurrection, there must first of all be death. Jesus died. We proclaim today that when Jesus died, we died. This is to say something strange and mysterious and past all finding out. To say that Jesus died is nothing — everybody dies, sooner or later. To say that Jesus died as an innocent martyr is to say little — many have died as martyrs to a cause. But to say Jesus died *for you*, this seems impossible! How can anyone die for anyone else? If there is one thing we must do absolutely alone, it is to die. How can the Gospel proclaim that Jesus died *for* us, when Christian churches keep burying their members one after the other? It is perfectly obvious that nobody dies *for* anybody. We, each of us, die for ourselves. Alone.

So it would seem. But death is more than a machine getting old, wearing out and breaking down, the cessation of physical activity. Human beings are not like automobiles. Every car eventually wears out and is junked, as we know only too well. Is that the way it is with people? No. People are alive and their bodies, by the wonders of God's preservation, keep renewing themselves. Unless I am mistaken, the human body is completely renewed every seven years or so. All the old cells die and new ones replace them again and again. Why then, suddenly, does the body stop renewing itself and begin to break down? Why must we die?

Jesus on the cross gives us God's answer — we die because of the judgment of God against our evil. "The wages of sin is death," the Bible says. "The soul that sinneth, it shall die." What God did at the time of Noah, destroying all humanity because of its wickedness, He is doing still today, one by one. One by one He is saying, "Depart from Me, ye workers of iniquity." But *that,* you see, is the death that Jesus died *for us.* The death which means the judgment of God against the sinner, His wrath and punishment, Jesus of Nazareth took in our place. "The Lord has laid on Him the iniquity of us all," Isaiah says. Instead of saying to us, "Depart from Me, you workers of iniquity," He said it to His own Son instead. I don't pretend to fully understand this. But I proclaim it to you as the truth of God: Christ Jesus has died for you! When you were baptized into Jesus, you died with Jesus on the cross. The penalty you have deserved for your evil-loving heart, for your evil deeds, for your failure to do what you ought has been suffered by Jesus Christ, the debt has been paid; He got what was coming to you. In Him you are dead!

So Be Dead to Sin

So be dead! God's Word says your "old self was crucified," your "sinful body is destroyed." We are no longer "enslaved to sin." We are "dead to sin." What does all that mean? Is it just the same old command, "Stop being bad, stop sinning," that we've probably heard over and over again ever since we can remember, and which hasn't been any more effective than telling a hunchback to stand up straight? No indeed! Saint Paul says, "Consider yourselves dead to sin!" That is to say, look, you are dead! Sin has done its worst to you. What more can it do besides kill you? And it has already done that when you, by Baptism, died with Christ on the cross. So now you don't have to be afraid of your sin or of God. You don't have to go around feeling guilty. You don't have to condemn yourself or punish yourself in any way.

It is like when you owe somebody some money and haven't paid it back for a long time. How do you feel when you see that person? You feel guilty and ashamed, don't you, and you do your best to avoid him? But when you have paid him back, you are free of the guilt, no longer do you have to avoid him or feel ashamed when you are around him. So it is with God. When we were sinners we felt guilty before God, we were afraid of Him, avoided Him, and even hated Him. But now the price has been paid. You have died for it with Christ! So now you are free! No more guilt, no more shame, no more avoiding God. Consider

yourselves dead to sin! It has already killed you!
It can't do anything more to you!

II. So Now We Rise with Christ

When He Rose We Rose

But don't leave it at that! Death has occurred
so there can be a resurrection! You are dead so
that you can come back to life. "We were buried
therefore with Him by Baptism into death, so that
as Christ was raised from the dead by the glory
of the Father, we too might walk in newness of
life." When Christ died you died. And when
Christ rose from the dead, so did you!

That's why it is so meaningful to baptize by
immersion. When you enter the water it is entering death with Christ. When the water closes
over your head you are dead and buried. But
when you come out of that water you are raised
from the dead into a whole new life! And that
is not just a symbol! That's what has happened
to you! It doesn't matter whether you were im-
mersed or sprinkled or however the water got on
you. The point is, we are raised from the dead
by Baptism.

St. Paul says Jesus was raised "by the glory
of the Father." By the glorious activity of God
He was given a new life. So God has acted on
you in your baptism and given you a new life.
It is like a television set. When it isn't plugged
in it is dead. When it is plugged in and has power

then it is alive to receive the television signals being broadcast from the studio. Our resurrection means that we are plugged into God, alive to Him, and His signals are moving us to action.

So Be Alive to God

So be alive to God! That's what Easter does to us, and unless it does that it avails us nothing. St. Paul says, "Consider yourselves alive to God." Look, you are alive! His signals are coming through to you! Tune in! His signals are saying to you, "I love you. I bought you to be My own by the death and resurrection of My Son. You are mine!" That signal transforms us into the images of God.

As a television set gives the image of the one broadcasting, so we become the images of God. We act like God acts. He loves the world — we love the world. He forgives sin — we forgive those who trespass against us. He heals and makes whole — we heal and help our neighbor. He saves the world — we proclaim that salvation to everyone. In short, to be raised from the dead means that we become like Jesus. As Jesus offered Himself as a sacrifice to God, so we offer ourselves as a living sacrifice, and God uses us as His instruments to love and serve the world. As Jesus offered Himself as the servant of all men, so we offer ourselves for our fellowmen, serving our neighbor wherever we are and in every way we can.

We are raised from the dead with Jesus and

are alive to God — tuned in to His signals. What a wonderful life that is! It's great to be alive, to be alive to God! The glory of the Father that raised Jesus from the dead is acting now on you! Be alive to those signals of mercy and love and forgiveness and power, and you'll be able to say, in every circumstance of life, it's great to be alive!